This Isn't Godhood

MS IKEJI

M.S Ikeji

Copyright © 2021 by M.S. Ikeji

All rights reserved. No part of this book may be reproduced in any manner whatsoever without written permission except in the case of brief quotations embodied in critical articles and reviews.

First Printing, 2021

THIS ISN'T GODHOOD

Contents

1
BACCHANALIA

2
MARIAN DEVOTIONS

3
YOUR UNFINISHED NOVEL

4
HANDS

5
ON SOLITUDE

6
SOL

7
WANTING

8
AMBROSIA

9
AFTER

Acknowledgements	41
About the Poet	43

1

Bacchanalia

Cry havoc! And let slip the gods of

Wine of

The sick sweet gorge of ripe figs find

The crush and thrum of

Blood, thick and potent enough to drink

Heated, and spiced such that you are overcome

By the delicious madness of Pan's flutes, a

March for joy and excess and the

Pulse of your hips

Frenzied as the spring

2

Marian Devotions

She says your name and you wonder if the deep bell

Toll of her voice will make her tongue taste like iron

Or the end of a vigil or the gold

Of her short, neatly filed nails. She kisses you.

Her tongue is pierced so it does taste metallic

And maybe this is what gold

Should taste like. So you drink her down,

Willing this moment to last until we are all consumed

By fire and water.

Her hand grips your jaw, holding your mouth a

Breath from her own. You plead, she pushes

Firm and gentle and inexorable as the end

Of the world until you lie prostrate before her, waiting

Patiently

For her to decide what comes next. She watches, you

Wait, shivering as she runs her fingernails

Up your thighs. She demands

Silence. You are silent. She touches

You, each whisper soft finger tempting gasps and

Sighs. You are silent. She

Grins. You shake, needy and silent. She

Waits. Your eyes beg, needy and silent. She

Buries herself in you and demands

Worship. You cry out in blasphemy, in

gratitude. You make

A litany of her name, make

A choir of your throat and hands and grasp at

Communion. *This is my body*

You say, *eat your fill.* She makes

You a private supper and you pray -

Spirit willing, flesh weak - that she

Never forsakes you. When she

Sinks her teeth into your side, water

Threatens to flow out of you, neither

Pure nor divine.

Finally, she lets you taste her metal

And flesh kiss again and when you're shaking

Breathless

Begging for salvation or judgement or the second coming she asks

What you want.

Bind me, you say. *Blind me. Teach me*

Humility and penance and a love of sacrifice.

Her teeth are a balm, her hands a scourge and you,

Something between a monk and a martyr revel in this

Surrendering of will and life giving

Fear. She is beautiful

And terrible, yet you trust her when she says

Do not be afraid

With her eyes that set you alight.

It is true then:

That not every prayer need be holy

And not every Mary divine

3

Your Unfinished Novel

I
She is hush soft, her breath barely stirring the air around you. Caught in the rose and resin scent of her, your eyes slide closed. She sighs, like a page turning.

II
When she chose you, in the sterile click and swipe which now passes for courtship, you imagined violets instead. Rewrote her profile in vellum and broad cursive, to match the lush excess of her hair and hips and gilded nose.

III
This moment hangs, suspended in the tension between verb and preposition. Just as you are about to snap, about to break this to comedy or tragedy, she

brings your mouths together in a press soft as a page turning.

IV

You fall into her, resolve the glide of her tongue into almost poems and the sharp edge of her teeth into nearly novels;

V

with her your heart is a typist crushed between sleepless caffeine and pitiless deadlines. Each beat presses her eyes *warm leather and ink* and her skin *ink and blackberries* and her moans *berries and whisky* into your eyes and palms and ear canals.

VI

Each beat fractures into something like a manuscript like

- the volumes drafted spread open on her bed
- the pages worn thin from her touch
- the margins and blank pages scribbled black with notes and addendums and appendices and

VII

together, your flesh could extend this moment into an age. You could show her the eight part epic you sketched between her fingers and your spine. You could be an author, co-author, editor, proofreader, ardent fan of the world woven between your lips.

VIII

Instead, you cradle her face, whisper your thumb across her cheek as your lips part. Her breath stirs yours, breaking the hush around you. There is nothing to stop this moment blurring into the next. Only breath, and scent, and the gold edging of a new page.

4

Hands

I want your hands
Nail to knucklebone

Slip your fingers between my lips and
Stroke me to the edge of reason or

Make me aware of the fragility of my skin
The slightest ounce of pressure to spill sensation into excess or

Use me to make mockery of gravity and art of
Corded silk and soft flesh

Let me rewrite protest to enticement and
Pain to ecstasy or

Call the flush in my cheeks and
Lost speech shame or

Let me feign chastity and
Play at modesty or

Make me a spectacle
A poor servant and fool's martyr to titillate your peers or

Deny me your hands and your teeth and your tongue to
Force silence or supplication

Sublimate my touch to yours
I am but a vessel for want
And wantonness and
Your desires
Twinned with mine

5

On Solitude

i do not think of him

ramming cervix deep or his

tongue against my jaw

i imagine

    breath

        misting a window

    a lover

        just out of reach

of their eyes

        begging for glass to be smoke

      their eyes

           hooded and focussed

of their voice

           muffled and indistinct,

of

hearing the plea in it

as   i gently circle my clit

     my breath comes faster

i whisper to them

     dying and living and drinking down the sight of me

          watch me

knowing   they cannot hear

     that glass is not smoke

     they want to know if i

          spoke or moaned

          taste sweet or salt

          am sun warm or dusk cool

i tease my nipple

               whisper soft and glacier patient

knowing   they   want and wait

                 are driven half mad

by   desire

    my skin

    my tongue flash pink against my teeth

       their hands curl as to grip my

             breast

                   waist

                         arse

they know

       i have made them to know

that they will not   taste musk

         know my skin is sweat warm

i move faster my

         core

        toes

                lips tightening

              heat building

they do not   hear me whimper

      feel the dry skin under my thighs

i am still   gentle

      patient

            pulling myself tight

                not thinking about him

      climbing

          wanted

              not being touched

      wanting

          touching

              surrounded by glass

            still

i am still

      on the edge of something beautiful

i am   beautiful

      releasing

my lover   does not exist

        was never needed

      only

          water and light

          a thousand sparks under my skin

i cannot breathe

i do not need breath,

      only

          water and light

          my fingers

              drawing this out

              carrying me across the abyss

i breathe

collapse

sweat damp and boneless

gloriously alone

6

Sol

Ask me to take you and

I will teach you how to lick away my corona;

it is the hottest part of me.

Roll my plasma between your fingertips.

Make me the centre of your universe.

Please,

give yourself to me. Let me nourish and mark you,

let me fill my hands with the soft expanse of you,

let me be your light and your heat. All I want

is your everything until you usher in the dusk and I,

tender as I can be, cradle you in my embers. Then

as night falls, as the burn cools and I am gone,

when the thought of me fills your mind and curls your tongue,

hold your hummingbird heart.

When it slicks your thighs and all you can do is

moan our memories into the dark,

answer the thrumming between them. But

do not disturb my fingerprints on the

rolls at your waist or lightning struck arms.

I'll be back in the morning, if you

ask me.

7

Wanting

Your eyes dip and linger for half a moment. My legs are barely contained by this too small chair and my too tight skirt. You frown, turn away, steal glances over your shoulder. It's OK, keep looking. I won't tell. Somehow, despite everything you've ever known and been taught and said, the oxblood curve of my lips and the lamp black gleam in my eye and the swell of flesh at my waist make your hands itch and your mouth go dry.

You won't speak to me, not with all these people around. You have an image to maintain, and somehow I doubt the adorable ginger on your arm will take too kindly to the questions you want to ask or the sigh that is simply dying to escape your lungs. The poor dear is already a little exasperated; you're so distracted, so distant. You best be a touch more attentive; you wouldn't want to ruin a good thing, not over someone like me. You won't forget though, and your eyes will find mine again before you leave for a night of adequate sex and inadequate sleep.

I stand to get a drink, and I can feel you watching me, devouring the sight of me: all soft fat and dark skin and sky high heels. You want more, because of course you do. You cannot begin to wrap your mind around why, because of course you can't. Do not try to comprehend, it will only make you angrier. You don't need to understand why you want to fill me and break me and learn my name in every language just so you can scream it. You only need to accept it, and accept that however much you want to possess me, it will only ever be a wanting. Try to claim the empty fantasy you think is contained in my wig and hips and velvet soft thighs and you will find teeth. You will find claws. You will find half a millenia of blood and malice itching to show you what you are.

But still, you're allowed to want me. I won't tell.

8

Ambrosia

I meet you at the apex of your thighs

Watch

    You quiver

    Your fingers

        Clench and release

Feel you

        Clench and release

Listen to every sucked breath and

Gentle moan like the

First hymn or herald to my

    Metamorphosis

You swear

    On my name

    Around my name

Need pouring from your lips into mine

But do gods need?

Could a mortal give ambrosia so freely?

Kiss me, maybe the answer is found in this

    Meeting of devotions

Perhaps I can decipher the

    Ridges on your teeth

    Texture of your tongue

Write a guide for all who would seek you

But if this cannot be learned in a moment

If I must spend a thousand years

    In study

    In contemplation

    In service

I will immerse myself in this most

Carnal priesthood

Praying that you

Choose me again.

9

After

you must be parched after that

I'll pop the kettle on

and make us popcorn

Sweet or salt?

    of course, always salt.

your spare bonnet is in the

top drawer

Are you hurt?

    Are you *bad* hurt?

I'll use the flogger next time

if you bring cake

        Anything but carrot, angel or fruit

here's some ice for your thighs

if you have it in you

        OK yes, *when* you have it in you

I just got a new strap I think you'll love

it's gorgeous

all blue and grey and soft as fuck

but first

What do you want to watch?

    ....fine

        but only because I love you.

Acknowledgements

This book couldn't have happened without so many people. These little note will be woefully incomplete, but I will try.

Thank you Jay, this book wouldn't have happened the way it did without you. Not only have you consistently encouraged (via bullying) my horniest tendencies, you drew the cover image and terrorised me in google doc comments. One of these days, we're gonna fight. I will lose. I am OK with this.

Thank you Shelby. Not only did you and Jay edit this collection, you edited my first real attempts to write about sex and always pushed me outside my comfort zone. Sol exists because of you. Your guidance and support has helped form me into the poet I am today.

Thank you to the Groupchat-Cum-Polycule. You're my family and my confidantes and I definitely wouldn't be the person I am without you. You've dealt with more panics, crises of confidence, and random bullshit than any reasonable group of people should have to. I couldn't ask for a better hype squad.

And thank you Twitter Black Romancelandia. I'm mostly a lurker, quietly liking your tweets and buying your books. Without your stories, fuelling my imagination, giving me language for desire and permission to create, I definitely wouldn't have been able to do this.

There are more people I haven't mentioned: people who support me in general, or my poetry specifically; people who've made me dinner or come to my shows or cheered at open mic nights; people who send me opportunities to get my work seen/me paid; people who listen to me rant/bitch/moan about things I can't be arsed trying to change. If I tried to name you all, I would definitely forget a whole bunch and these acknowledgements would be longer than the book itself. Suffice to say, I see you and I love you.

I hope this pamphlet is just the beginning, and I continue to write about sex and desire. If I do, know that it is because of these wonderful people. If I don't, know that it's because I have studiously ignored their advice.

Art by Jay Delise

About the Poet

M.S. Ikeji is a poet and performer whose work is probably best described as something akin to John Keats with a top lip and bigger ass.

Other personal information of note includes: they're a 2nd gen Nigerian immigrant, hopelessly untidy and a bisexual Virgo.

Find them on twitter @MazHedgehog